Withdrawn

CREATIVE EDUCATION

JULIE NELSON

OAKLAND RAIDERS

Published by Creative Education
123 South Broad Street, Mankato, Minnesota 56001
Creative Education is an imprint of The Creative Company

Designed by Rita Marshall

Photos by: Allsport USA, Bettmann/CORBIS, SportsChrome

Library of Congress Cataloging-in-Publication Data

Nelson, Julie.
Oakland Raiders / by Julie Nelson.
p. cm. — (NFL today)
Summary: Traces the history of the Oakland Raiders from the team's
beginnings through 1999.
ISBN 1-58341-054-6

1. Oakland Raiders (Football team)—History—Juvenile literature.
[1. Oakland Raiders (Football team)—History. 2. Football—History.]
I. Title. II. Series: NFL today (Mankato, Minn.)

GV956.024N45   2000
796.332'64'0979466—dc21   99-023742

First edition

9 8 7 6 5 4 3 2 1

The city of Oakland, California, sits along the east side of the San Francisco Bay. Founded in 1854 during the great California gold rush, Oakland grew slowly and always seemed to be overshadowed by San Francisco, its larger sister city across the bay. But Oakland's professional football team, the Raiders of the National Football League, has never played second fiddle to any team.

Since their start in 1960, the Oakland Raiders have become one of the NFL's most prestigious teams. The list of Raiders stars is a long one that includes quarterbacks George Blanda and Ken Stabler; receivers Fred Biletnikoff and Tim

Hall of Fame receiver Fred Biletnikoff.

Brown; running backs Marcus Allen and Bo Jackson; linebacker Ted Hendricks; and defensive end Howie Long.

Guided by legendary owner Al Davis, the Raiders appeared in Super Bowls in each of their first three decades and have won the world championship three times. With their intimidating black uniforms and logo and their reputation for aggressive play, the Oakland Raiders have also created a mystique that makes them one of the NFL's most feared and captivating teams.

1 9 6 1

Rugged center Jim Otto was named to the AFL's All-League team for the second straight season.

THE MAN BEHIND THE SILVER AND BLACK

For nearly 40 years, Al Davis has been the man behind the Raiders organization. Since he took over the losing franchise in 1963, his hard work, intelligence, and energy have taken Oakland to the top.

Davis began his pro football career as an assistant coach with the San Diego Chargers. During his time in San Diego, he helped build the Chargers into one of the most feared passing teams in football.

Davis soon saw a greater challenge in Oakland, and the young coach moved there in 1963 to take over the floundering Oakland Raiders. Oakland, the last city to get an American Football League franchise, was starving for good players and leadership. One of the few players who was a steady presence for the Raiders would go on to become a legend: center Jim Otto. Many Raiders fans remember his name, but they also remember him by his jersey number: "00."

In the Raiders' first training camp, Otto immediately became a team leader. Some veteran NFL players wondered

One of the NFL's finest cornerbacks, Charles Woodson.

why such a talented player would sign with an AFL team. "I could make some NFL clubs, I know," said Otto, "but it's more of an honor and distinction to be an original member of a brand new league. That's why I chose to play with the Oakland Raiders." There wasn't much honor or success for Otto during the team's first three seasons, however. The Raiders won only nine of the 33 games they played in 1960, 1961, and 1962.

The Raiders needed some inspiration, and it came in the form of 34-year-old Al Davis, who arrived in Oakland full of energy and new ideas. "Poise is the secret," Davis told his new team. "No matter what the scoreboard says, keep your poise." In 1963, Davis's first season, the Raiders rocketed to a 10–4 record, just barely missing the AFL playoffs.

Other team owners in the AFL noticed Davis's winning attitude. To give the AFL an edge over its rival, the National Football League, the owners made Davis the commissioner of the American Football League in April 1966.

Davis resigned from his new post just 10 weeks later after putting an end to the six-year struggle between the AFL and NFL. The two leagues formed an alliance, and Davis returned to the Raiders as general manager. Although his coaching career was over, he continued to strive for the same goal: making the Raiders into world champions.

1 9 6 7

Under general manager Al Davis, the Raiders roared to a 13–1 record and the AFL title.

A COMMITMENT TO EXCELLENCE

With the two leagues united, a true world champion could finally be crowned, and the Raiders wanted that crown. On January 14, 1968, in the second NFL-AFL

Super Bowl, the Raiders met the mighty Green Bay Packers, who were coached by the legendary Vince Lombardi.

"Seven years ago, I thought this day would never come," Jim Otto said proudly. "We are in the Super Bowl." In only seven years, the Raiders had risen from doormats to Super Bowl contenders—from playing games on a high school field during their opening season to battling for the world championship. In the Super Bowl, Raiders coach John Rauch tried several strategies, but his young team was no match for Lombardi's veterans. Green Bay pulled away to win 33–14.

Three years after their first Super Bowl appearance, as the 1960s came to an end, the Raiders had established themselves as one of pro football's best teams. Such standouts as receivers Bill Miller and Fred Biletnikoff, quarterbacks George Blanda and Daryle Lamonica, and defensive back Willie Brown made Oakland one of the league's strongest and most well-balanced teams. Oakland ended the decade in 1969 with a sensational 12–1–1 season.

The Raiders continued to dominate during their second decade. A burly new coach ushered in a new era in Raiders football in the 1970s. That coach, John Madden, rewrote the book on effective coaching in the NFL. "I had a philosophy," Madden explained. "I really liked my players. I liked them as people. I made a point to talk to each player personally every day. . . . You can be intense and competitive and all that, but try to remember to laugh and have fun. It's just a football game."

Madden instilled this philosophy in his team. His Raiders became famous for their ability to secure victories in unusual ways with remarkable players. One of these football magi-

1 9 7 1

John Madden led Oakland to its seventh straight winning season (8–4–2).

9

Quarterback Ken "the Snake" Stabler.

All-Pro defensive tackle Chester McGlockton.

Quarterback Ken Stabler had a great season, passing for 2,469 yards and 26 touchdowns.

cians was Ken "the Snake" Stabler, the Raiders' hard-throwing, left-handed quarterback.

Stabler picked up his nickname in high school after zigzagging across the football field like a snake as he returned a punt for a touchdown. He later quarterbacked the University of Alabama Crimson Tide team under coaching legend Bear Bryant.

As the Raiders' quarterback, Stabler's greatest asset was his quick throwing release. In 1972, he led the league in passing, and Oakland's 10–3–1 record landed the Raiders in the playoffs. They were only seconds away from beating Pittsburgh when Steelers running back Franco Harris pulled off his famous "Immaculate Reception" play to seal a 13–7 Pittsburgh win in the first round.

In 1973, the Raiders were back, as Stabler and a powerful Oakland defense led the team to a 9–4–1 record. This time, the Raiders got revenge against Pittsburgh by thrashing the Steelers 33–14 in the playoffs. The Miami Dolphins, however, then kept the Raiders from the Super Bowl, beating Oakland 27–10 in the AFC championship game.

The next two seasons, the Raiders again made the playoffs but failed to capture the championship. As the 1976 season began, Coach Madden placed the team's future in Ken Stabler's hands. With help from such outstanding receivers as Dave Casper, Cliff Branch, and Fred Biletnikoff, Stabler made 1976 a season to remember. With each game, the confident Raiders seemed to grow stronger, building up a league-best 13–1 record.

In the playoffs, though, it looked like history might repeat itself. Oakland again faced the Pittsburgh Steelers, the team that had ended the Raiders' march toward the Super Bowl three times. But this time, Oakland crushed the overmatched Steelers 27–7. Only one more team, the Minnesota Vikings, stood between Oakland and its first world championship.

Minnesota, featuring the renowned "Purple People Eaters" defensive front row, was indeed a team to be feared. But Oakland's Fred Biletnikoff pulled in several long passes at key moments as the Raiders ran away to a 33–14 win. Biletnikoff was named the game's Most Valuable Player for his heroics, and the Raiders walked off the field with their first Super Bowl championship. John Madden, the coach whom George Blanda had once called "the kindest and most thoughtful coach I ever had," finally had the Super Bowl trophy he had worked so long for.

1 9 7 8

Veteran receiver Fred Biletnikoff caught his 76th touchdown pass—a team record.

THE TRADITION CONTINUES

In 1978, after compiling a career 103–32–7 record, John Madden left the Raiders and moved into sports broadcasting. When Tom Flores became Oakland's new skipper, he found a team eager to again climb to championship heights.

Like most students of the game, Flores knew of Oakland's reputation as a place where football's troublemakers, outcasts, and aging veterans came to end their pro careers. When Flores arrived in Oakland, he found quarterback Jim Plunkett, one such former star, sitting on the bench.

Plunkett had been a promising college player who never played to his potential after turning pro. Flores, however, thought that he detected a spark of the ambition and talent that once drove Plunkett, so he put his faith in the veteran quarterback. What followed was one of the most amazing personal comebacks in football history.

After the Raiders lost three of their first five games in 1980, Flores sent Plunkett into the game as the permanent starter. The move paid off immediately. Plunkett quarterbacked Oakland to nine wins in its next 11 games. By the season's end, the Raiders had made the playoffs as a Wild Card team. The Raiders continued their improbable run by beating Houston, Cleveland, and San Diego to reach the Super Bowl.

1 9 8 0

Jim Plunkett won the starting quarterback position and tossed 18 touchdown passes.

Few football experts gave Oakland much of a chance against the powerful Philadelphia Eagles, and Plunkett and the Raiders' defense—led by cornerback Lester Hayes—went into Super Bowl XV feeling they had nothing to lose. Plunkett completed 13 of 21 passes, including an incredible 80-yard touchdown bomb to Kenny King. The Raiders left the field in New Orleans that day as Super Bowl champions, having trounced Philadelphia 27–10.

The 1982 NFL draft brought Heisman Trophy-winning running back Marcus Allen, out of the nearby University of Southern California, to Oakland. Allen, who would go on to set team records for career rushing yards (8,545) and total touchdowns (95), was just the offensive weapon Plunkett needed to balance the passing attack. It appeared that the Raiders had the offensive combination they needed to further their championship glory in the 1980s.

THE RAIDERS HEAD SOUTH

In 1982, the Raiders decided to leave Oakland and move south to Los Angeles. The Raiders loved Oakland and its

14

Longtime star halfback Marcus Allen.

Sure-handed tight end Todd Christensen.

fans, but the city's stadium seated only 50,000 spectators—Davis believed that his team could draw at least 90,000 fans per game in Los Angeles. Although the NFL tried to block the move, Davis took his team south for the 1982 season after receiving permission in court.

Once the Raiders were situated in their new home, they kicked off the 1982 season with three straight wins. Marcus Allen's outstanding season helped draw attention to the new team in town. He rushed for 697 yards in his rookie year, averaging 5.7 yards per carry and scoring 14 touchdowns. For his accomplishments, Allen was named Rookie of the Year.

Allen again led the team in rushing in 1983 with 1,014 yards. Jim Plunkett also had a fine year, throwing for 2,935 yards and 20 touchdowns. Led by a great offensive line, the Raiders carried a 12–4 record into the postseason, then powered their way to the Super Bowl. In that championship spotlight, Allen turned in a performance that devastated the opposing Washington Redskins defense and astounded fans around the country.

When the Raiders had faced Washington earlier in the year, they had come up short in a 37–35 decision. This time, however, the Raiders' offense overpowered the Redskins, while the Oakland defense limited Washington to only one touchdown and one field goal enroute to a lopsided 38–9 victory. Marcus Allen pummeled the Washington defense, carrying the ball 20 times for a record 191 yards, including a 74-yard scoring run. Raiders right guard Mickey Marvin remembered seeing Allen rush by him on the long run. "I was picking myself up off the ground," Marvin recalled, "then I looked around and a rocket went through."

1 9 8 3

Fierce defensive end Greg Townsend played the first season of his 11-year Raiders career.

Intimidating defensive end Howie Long (pages 18-19).

The rocket, of course, was the speedy Allen, who almost single-handedly led the Raiders to their third world championship. "This has to be the greatest feeling of my life," Allen said after the game. "I've been to the Rose Bowl. I've won the Heisman Trophy. But nothing is sweeter than this."

THE BO JACKSON EXPRESS

Coach Tom Flores retired after the 1987 season, and Al Davis soon chose offensive line coach Art Shell as the team's new head coach. Shell had Raiders blood running through his veins. Many Raiders fans consider Shell—who wore the silver and black from 1968 to 1982—to be the best offensive tackle to ever play the game. He went to the Pro Bowl eight times and played in 207 league games over 15 seasons. One of the most respected men in football, Shell quickly earned the trust and loyalty of his players.

A winning NFL coach, however, needs more than just respect. He needs talented, disciplined, and hardworking players, and no one embodied those characteristics more than Shell's star running back, Bo Jackson.

Vincent Edward Jackson was born in Bessemer, Alabama. The eighth of 10 children, he was an energetic and fearless youngster whom his family and friends described as being wild as a "boarhog." From this comparison came Jackson's abbreviated nickname: "Bo."

Everyone knew that Jackson had exceptional athletic talent. He won the Heisman Trophy in 1985 as a running back at Auburn. Instead of joining the NFL, however, Jackson chose a second option—playing professional baseball for the Kansas City Royals. Two years later, Al Davis acquired the rights to Jackson in the seventh round of the NFL draft. Many fans and sportswriters thought Davis had wasted a draft pick. No one, they claimed, could play two professional sports in the same season.

Once Bo decided to split his time between the two sports, he soon proved that he could not only play football, but dominate the sport. In a 1987 Monday night game against Seattle, with all of America watching, Bo ran for an incredible 221 yards, including a spectacular 90-yard run.

Although a hip injury cut his football career short in 1990, Jackson had already secured a reputation as one of the most electrifying runners in NFL history. In just three seasons, he set new Raiders records for most yards per carry (5.4) and

Jay Schroeder took over as Oakland's new quarterback, throwing 13 touchdown passes.

Safety Eddie Anderson anchored the Raiders defense.   21

Bo Jackson's combination of speed and power was unmatched.

most rushing yards in a single game (221). He also became the only NFL player to ever have two runs of more than 90 yards (91 and 92).

RAIDERS PRIDE

During Art Shell's five-year coaching stint in Los Angeles, the Raiders missed the playoffs only once. Then, in 1994, the Raiders beat Denver 42–24 to win the AFC Wild Card game and draw within two games of a Super Bowl berth. Their hopes of a return visit to the Super Bowl disappeared, however, when they journeyed to Buffalo. The Raiders had a hard time adjusting from southern California's warm weather to Buffalo's frigid winter, and the Bills pulled out a 29–23 victory.

In 1995, owner Al Davis decided to pack up and move his Raiders back to Oakland after a 13-year absence. The franchise also hired Mike White, a Raiders assistant coach, as the team's new head coach. The Raiders finished the 1995 season with an 8–8 record, a respectable showing in the tough AFC Western Division. Oakland fans cared little about the record, though—they were happy just to have their beloved Raiders back home.

The Raiders slumped the next two seasons, failing to make the playoffs or even finish above the .500 mark. Oakland slipped to 7–9 in 1996 and plummeted to 4–12 the following season. Although they lacked the talent to contend for a Super Bowl title, the Raiders did have two offensive weapons that kept the team exciting: Napoleon Kaufman and Tim Brown.

Jeff Hostetler helped right the Raiders ship, leading Oakland to a 10–6 finish.

Kaufman, a first-round draft pick out of the University of Washington in 1995, began his pro career in Oakland as mainly a kick returner. It wasn't until 1997 that he became a full-time starter at the halfback position. At only 5-foot-9 and 185 pounds, Kaufman had to earn the respect of opposing defenses by proving his toughness. "People will have their questions about my durability," he said. "I've dealt with it through high school, college, and now in the pros. . . . I just fight when I get the ball."

Kaufman emerged as a star in 1997, gaining 1,294 yards with his breakaway speed and great agility. In one game against Denver, he tore through the Broncos defense for 227 yards, including an 83-yard touchdown dash. "He's got incredible speed," marveled Broncos linebacker Bill Ro-

1 9 9 6

Tackle Chester McGlockton led the club with eight quarterback sacks.

Cornerback Terry McDaniel starred in Oakland for 10 years.

manowski. "With a guy like him, you break down defensively and he'll rip you apart."

The Raiders' other main offensive force was Tim Brown, a veteran wide receiver who had first donned a silver and black uniform in 1988. After 10 years with the Raiders, Brown had put together six straight 1,000-yard seasons, earned seven Pro Bowl appearances, and become the franchise's all-time leader in receiving yards.

Brown, Kaufman, and quarterback Jeff George, a new arrival, all had superb seasons in 1997, but Oakland still fell to 4–12—its worst finish since 1962. Despite the strong play of tackle Chester McGlockton and safety Eric Turner, the Raiders' defense finished dead last in the NFL, and new head coach Joe Bugel survived only one season.

1 9 9 7

Jeff George set team records in passing yards (3,917) and touchdowns (29).

QUEST FOR THE CROWN

In hopes of turning around his once-proud franchise, Al Davis made several key moves in preparation for the 1998 season. The first was to hire Philadelphia offensive coordinator Jon Gruden, who, at the age of 34, became the youngest active head coach in the NFL. "I like Jon's passion, his resiliency," said Davis. "I got the feeling that he has something that we need."

Another man who had what the Raiders needed was rookie defensive back Charles Woodson. A three-year starting cornerback for the University of Michigan, Woodson had become the first primarily defensive player ever to win the Heisman Trophy. While competing against such standouts as quarterback Peyton Manning and receiver Randy Moss in the

Napoleon Kaufman shredded defenses with his speed (pages 26-27).

Quarterback Rich Gannon was named to the Pro Bowl after passing for 24 touchdowns.

Heisman voting, Woodson was not afraid to make clear who he thought deserved the nod. "The best player in the country is standing before you," he told reporters.

Woodson could also run the ball, catch passes, and return kicks, but it was his defensive play that earned him the Heisman Trophy. Later that year, to shore up their sagging defense, the Raiders selected him with their top draft pick, making him the seventh former Heisman winner to play for Oakland. "He's after the next adventure, and he's going to get it here," Gruden said. "He's a legitimate future star cornerback in this league."

Woodson's impact in Oakland was immediate. Led by Woodson, linebacker Greg Biekert, and defensive end Lance Johnstone, the Raiders' defense emerged as one of the best in football in 1998. Woodson's 62 tackles and five interceptions earned him NFL Defensive Rookie of the Year honors.

Still, despite some individual bright spots and an improved attitude in the locker room, Oakland failed to make the playoffs in 1998. Injuries and an inconsistent offense dropped the Raiders to an 8–8 finish after a 7–3 start.

The Raiders' first order of business after the season was to stabilize their quarterback situation. After throwing for a league-leading 3,917 yards in 1997, Jeff George had struggled in 1998 and was released. The Raiders next put their faith in veteran quarterback Rich Gannon, who had spent time with several NFL teams before landing in Oakland.

Another key acquisition was big running back Tyrone Wheatley. Although the former Michigan star had struggled in his first few years with the New York Giants, the move to Oakland seemed to reenergize his career. Wheatley ran for

Guard Steve Wisniewski, a perennial All-Pro.

Amazing receiver and punt returner Tim Brown.

Huge defensive tackle Darrell Russell.

The Raiders looked for end Regan Upshaw to add speed to their defensive line.

more than 900 yards in 1999, teaming up with Kaufman to give the Raiders both power and speed in the backfield.

Gannon also had one of his finest seasons, passing for nearly 4,000 yards as the Raiders went 8–8. Although the Raiders struggled in close games—losing all eight times by seven points or less—the season did produce one memorable win. Late in the year, Oakland dealt a strong Tampa Bay team a 45–0 drubbing. The margin of victory was Oakland's largest since joining the NFL in 1970. "I think there's progress being made," Coach Gruden said. "[W]e're a better football team this year than we were last year without a doubt."

Today's Raiders are a team to be feared. With the addition of strong-legged kicker Sebastian Janikowski—the team's top pick in the 2000 draft—the men in silver and black have plenty of firepower. With such stars as Charles Woodson leading the way, today's Raiders are ready to become the best in the AFC West again.